DEVON GARDENS

SALMON

INTRODUCTION

The British passion for gardens and gardening has developed through many centuries, and the county of Devon has an unsurpassed variety of magnificent gardens set amidst a glorious backdrop of rolling green hills, stunning seascapes and delightful villages. Here can be seen every type of garden from the flamboyant formal gardens and sweeping lawns associated with historic houses and stately homes to the intimate and colourful cottage garden. Devon's mild climate provides a wonderful opportunity for seeing plants which do not thrive in other parts of the country, including many exotic species brought from around the world by the great 19th century plant collectors. It was they who transformed the English garden by bringing rhododendrons, azaleas, camellias and magnolias to these shores as well as the subtropical ferns and palms which flourish in the west country. From the eagerly awaited first snowdrops of spring, which comes early to Devon, to the vibrant colours of lingering, warm autumn days, there is much to delight and inspire visitors throughout the entire year.

Broomhill Sculpture Garden

MARWOOD HILL, near Barnstaple

A mature garden, but one that is constantly being augmented and updated, Marwood Hill near Barnstaple contains more than 5,000 different varieties of plants in a splendid valley setting. It is known for its magnificent flowering shrubs as well as plantings of willows, ferns and eucalyptus. The gardens also feature a pergola with twelve varieties of wisteria, three small lakes, a bog garden and a glasshouse containing an exceptional collection of camellias. Marwood Hill holds three National Collections: Japanese iris, tulbaghia, related to the onion and a native of Africa, and a near-complete collection of the many varieties of astilbes.

DEVON GARDENS

KNIGHTSHAYES COURT, near Tiverton

A grand country house begun in 1869, Knightshayes Court has one of the finest gardens in Devon with acres of parkland and woodland overlooking the valley of the River Exe. The gardens, which contain many rare plants and some unique topiary, have been largely re-created in the last half century. The formal gardens are situated on a steep slope below the house, and here there are terraces, herbaceous borders and lawns. A battlemented yew hedge encloses the Pool Garden with its lily pond. Now owned by The National Trust, Knightshayes has some fine specimen trees, and there are delightful woodland walks.

DEVON GARDENS

12

KNIGHTSHAYES COURT

13

COLETON FISHACRE, Kingswear

Situated in a sheltered combe on a beautiful stretch of the South Devon coast, Coleton Fishacre house and garden has a fine collection of rare and exotic plants, as well as unusual trees such as the dawn redwood, swamp cypress and Chilean myrtle. Streams and ponds help to create a humid atmosphere in which some superb bamboos and mimosas flourish. The formal walls and terraces which surround the house offer ideal protection for tender, sun-loving plants. Created in the 1920s by a pupil of the famous architect and designer Sir Edwin Lutyens, the house and garden are now in the care of The National Trust.

BROOMHILL SCULPTURE GARDEN, Muddiford

Situated in a beautiful woodland setting with a stream and a trout lake, Broomhill Sculpture Garden has been developed over the last ten years on the site of gardens which had been neglected for many decades. Scattered around the ten-acre site are 300 works by sculptors of international renown, all superbly integrated with the natural environment, and reached by winding paths through the woods and around the lake. The gardens themselves provide interest throughout the year but they are especially lovely in spring when there is a splendid array of snowdrops, daffodils, primroses and bluebells as well as flowering shrubs.

DEVON GARDENS

BURROW FARM GARDENS, near Axminster

These delightful gardens in the east of the county have been largely created over the last 40 years from pasture land. The fascinating woodland garden occupies the site of an ancient Roman clay pit where an extensive bog garden is surrounded by wild flowers early in the year. In summer, colourful herbaceous plants and old-fashioned varieties of rose decorate the pergola walk, while the courtyard and terraced gardens, with their later-flowering plants, continue to provide interest as the year progresses. A new addition for the millennium, the rill garden has a traditional stone summer-house and a water feature.

DEVON GARDENS

TORRE ABBEY, Torquay

Originally founded as a monastery in 1196, Torre Abbey is Torquay's oldest building, currently undergoing a major restoration. Only one of the three gatehouses is still standing and many of the buildings were later converted into a private residence. The remains of the abbey are surrounded by extensive grounds which include colourful flower-beds, a superb lawn with scattered trees, rock and water gardens and even palm and cacti houses. The Spanish Barn, so called because Spanish prisoners from the Armada were housed there, provides an ideal setting for occasional flower shows, festivals and plant sales.

DOCTON MILL, Lymebridge near Hartland

As this garden occupies the site of a derelict Saxon water-mill, water is an important feature of the design at Docton Mill. Here a river, small streams, ponds and leats provide ideal conditions for water-loving plants such as ligularias, primulas and ferns. When this garden was first created in the 1980s, the intention was to make a natural display which integrated cultivated areas with the wild. The result is a magnificent array of traditional spring flowers such as bluebells, primulas and narcissi which grow alongside the more exotic camellias, azaleas and magnolias. In summer, the colour and scent of roses fills the garden.

DEVON GARDENS

DOCTON MILL

CASTLE DROGO, Drewsteignton

Begun in 1910, Castle Drogo was the last castle to be built in England and its designer, Sir Edwin Lutyens, was also responsible for the layout of the gardens. Occupying a moorland spur above the River Teign, Castle Drogo offers magnificent views over Dartmoor and the Teign Gorge. The wooded valley is richly planted wth flowering shrubs and trees while the formal, terraced gardens feature spring bulbs, herbs and herbaceous borders planted with many old varieties of traditional cottage garden flowers such as montbretia, iris and red-hot pokers. The splendid circular lawn is sheltered by a tall yew hedge.

DARTINGTON HALL, near Totnes

A 14th century tilt-yard, flanked by banks and terraces, lies at the heart of the magnificent restored gardens at Dartington Hall. Here rows of ancient trees, including chestnut and yew, provide a backdrop for modern sculptures by artists including Henry Moore and Peter Randall-Page. There are three walkways where bay, yew and holly plantings provide a contrast to flowering trees and shrubs such as camellias, magnolias and rhododendrons. A more recent addition, the Japanese garden offers a tranquil area for quiet contemplation, and is recognised as one of the most outstanding Japanese gardens in the United Kingdom.

DARTINGTON HALL

ESCOT HOUSE, near Ottery St. Mary

The vast parkland estate which surrounds Escot House extends over 220 acres and was originally laid out by Capability Brown. Today it offers a unique opportunity to experience nature and wildlife, sympathetically managed in a superb location in the south-east of the county. Woodland walks, nature trails and beautiful vistas are complemented by a fine collection of specimen trees, shrubs and flowers. Recent developments include a wetlands centre, created from the old ice ponds, and a collection of birds of prey. Unusual animals which also inhabit the park are Asian otters, the increasingly rare native red squirrel and wild boar.

ARLINGTON COURT, near Barnstaple

The gardens at Georgian Arlington Court are largely informal with spring bulbs and wild flowers carpeting the grass, and a wilderness area where rhododendrons and hydrangeas thrive in the mild, damp climate and acid soil. In contrast, the formal, terraced Victorian garden has a rockery, a conservatory and an ornamental pond. Beyond the garden there are superb walks in the historic parkland where Jacob sheep and Shetland ponies graze at will, and a lake provides ideal conditions for bird-watchers. The house is in the ownership of The National Trust, and the stables contain a large collection of 19th century horse-drawn vehicles.

OVERBECKS MUSEUM AND GARDEN, near Salcombe

Owned in the early 20th century by scientist Otto Overbeck, this National Trust property contains many items relating to his life and interests. The beautiful garden, which offers spectacular views over the Salcombe estuary and enjoys a mild, damp climate, is home to many rare and exotic plants, trees and shrubs. Among the more unusual are a large camphor tree, a Himalayan magnolia which is more than one hundred years old and huge fruiting banana palms. Orange and lemon trees are planted in the classical parterre which achieves some delightful effects by the use of coloured gravel, edged with box.

KILLERTON HOUSE, Broadclyst near Exeter

Featuring a costume collection and a Victorian laundry, 18th century Killerton House is set in fifteen acres of beautiful gardens surrounded by parkland, woods and farmland. Killerton is noted for its magnificent trees which include a beech avenue, Wellingtonias, Lawson cypresses, oaks, maples and the largest tulip tree in England. Many of the trees were planted when the garden was created in the 1770s. The garden has something of interest for every season: banks of rhododendrons and magnolias cover the hillside in spring, bedding plants provide summer colour, and the mature trees are especially lovely in autumn.

KILLERTON HOUSE

HARTLAND ABBEY

This former Augustinian monastery is set in a narrow, sheltered valley within a designated Area of Outstanding Natural Beauty, only a mile from Devon's spectacular Atlantic coast. Garden designer Gertrude Jekyll was an occasional guest at the abbey and she is thought to be responsible for some of the design, including the fernery. Built on the sides of the valley to avoid the prevailing winds, a series of walled gardens is stocked with herbaceous plants, roses, clematis and vegetables. A spectacular show is provided in spring and early summer by the profusion of azaleas, rhododendrons, camellias, hydrangeas and gunnera.

PECORAMA, Beer

Situated on the hillside above the picturesque fishing village of Beer, Pecorama offers a wide range of attractions and activities. Home to the Beer Heights Light Railway, the gardens also offer some stunning horticultural features, including the innovative Peco Millennium Garden. Here a series of themed gardens, linked by scented walkways, includes a roof garden enclosed within a ruined tower, and a moat garden from which water trickles down to the brightly coloured flower-beds of the Rainbow Garden. Contrasting with the Sun Garden's vibrant yellows and golds, the Moon Garden is planted with shades of silver and blue.

TAPELEY PARK, Instow

Standing at the end of a long drive lined by trees and flowering shrubs, this impressive 17th century mansion overlooks the estuary of the Rivers Taw and Torridge near Bideford. The extensive garden descends from the house in a series of ornamental terraces to a ravine where the lake is surrounded by huge thuja *plicata* trees which are the oldest of their kind in the country. Colourful native plants, such as roses, lavenders, primroses and primulas, contrast with more exotic species including yuccas, agapanthus and mimosa. Among the other features of the garden are an ilex tunnel, a shell house and an ice house.

COCKINGTON COURT, near Torquay

Situated in a valley between the popular Devon Riviera resorts of Torquay and Paignton, Cockington is a picturesque hamlet of thatched, cob-walled cottages. The epitome of the peaceful rural charm of old England, the village attracts many photographers and artists. Cockington Court is set in a 450-acre park with a cricket pitch, historic church and ornamental lakes. The house, which now contains a craft centre, was rebuilt in 1679 and it was at this time that the gardens were created. These include an organic garden and the beautiful, walled rose garden which provides a sheltered, tranquil haven behind the court.

ROSEMOOR, Great Torrington

Superbly situated in the scenic Torridge valley, Rosemoor was the Royal Horticultural Society's first regional garden, acquired in 1988, and it contains an outstanding variety of flowering trees, shrubs, herbaceous plants and bulbs. A winding gorge planted with ferns and bamboos links an arboretum and a lake to the formal garden with its colour themed 'hot' square and 'cool' spiral gardens. Fruit, vegetables and herbs flourish here, and other attractions include a winter garden, a foliage garden and a cottage garden. Rosemoor is particularly noted for its rose gardens which have over 2,000 roses from 200 varieties.

INDEX

Printed and published by J. Salmon Ltd., 100 London Road, Sevenoaks, Kent.
Telephone: 01732 452381   Email: enquiries@jsalmon.co.uk   Website: www.jsalmon.co.uk

ISBN 1 84640 029 5
Photographs by Chris Wormald

Arlington Court ●

Broomhill Sculpture Garden
●
● Marwood Hill

● Tapeley Park

Docton Mill ●
●
Hartland Abbey

● Rosemoor

● Knightshayes
Court

Killerton House ●

Burrow Farm ●

Castle Drogo ●

Escot House ●
● Pecorama

Cockington Court ●
● Torre Abbey

Dartington Hall ●
● Coleton Fishacre

● Overbecks